T

CW00689760

Compiled and Edited
by Rudrangshu Mukherjee

PENGUIN BOOKS

PENGUIN BOOKS

Published by the Penguin Group

Penguin Books India Pvt Ltd, 11 Community Centre, Panchsheel Park, New Delhi
110 017, India
Penguin Group (USA) Inc., 375 Hudson Street, New York, New York 10014, USA
Penguin Group (Canada), 10 Alcorn Avenue, Toronto, Ontario, Canada M4V
3B2 (a division of Pearson Penguin Canada Inc.)
Penguin Books Ltd, 80 Strand, London WC2R 0RL, England
Penguin Ireland, 25 St Stephen's Green, Dublin 2, Ireland (a division of Penguin
Books Ltd)
Penguin Group (Australia), 250 Camberwell Road, Camberwell, Victoria 3124,
Australia (a division of Pearson Australia Group Pty Ltd)
Penguin Group (NZ), cnr Airborne and Rosedale Road, Albany, Auckland 1310,
New Zealand (a division of Pearson New Zealand Ltd)
Penguin Group (South Africa) (Pty) Ltd, 24 Sturdee Avenue, Rosebank,
Johannesburg 2196, South Africa

Penguin Books Ltd, Registered Offices: 80 Strand, London WC2R 0RL, England

First published by Penguin Books India 1999

Copyright © H.H. The Dalai Lama 1999

Typeset in Futura by Digital Technologies and Printing Solutions, New Delhi
Printed at Saurabh Printers Pvt. Ltd, Noida

Introduction

In a century in which the virtues of western culture and civilization have more or less been taken for granted, the ideas of Mohandas Karamchand Gandhi offer a radical alternative. He considered a society based on industrialism to be violent and therefore satanic. He located the strength of India in the villages and in the long tradition of ahimsa. In an age torn by violence and destruction, Gandhi's creed of non-violence is a message for survival. His message was utopian; however, without dreams there can be no responsibilities. Some of Gandhi's sayings are presented in this Little Book. Without their context, Gandhi's words might appear idiosyncratic. But if this book leads readers to the writings of Gandhi, it will have served its purpose; for reading Gandhi— even for those who disagree with him—is always rewarding.

I go to discover means
whereby I can give you
the faith that is in me.

I believe in non-violent communism.

For me non-violence is something to be
shunned if it is a private virtue.
My concept of non-violence is universal.
It belongs to the millions.

Truth is its own proof, and
non-violence is its supreme fruit.

If national life becomes so perfect as to become self-regulated, no representation is necessary. There is then a state of enlightened anarchy.

Non-violence is the supreme dharma;
there is no discovery of greater import
than this.

He who can restrain the senses
is a man of self-control; but the man
whose senses have become, through
constant practice, incapable of enjoying
their objects, has transcended
self-control, has in fact attained moksha.

We should get our peace
not from the external environment, but
from within us.

The voice of the people should be
the voice of God.

The royal road is the doing of one's appointed duty to the best of one's ability and the dedication of all services to God.

God is invisible, beyond the reach of the human eye. All that we can do, therefore, is to try to understand the words and actions of those whom we regard as men of God.

Let me explain what I mean by religion.
It is not the Hindu religion . . . but the
religion which transcends Hinduism,
which changes one's very nature, which
binds one indissolubly to the truth within
and which ever purifies.

The individual, being pure,
sacrifices himself for the family,
the latter for the village, the village
for the district, the district for the
province, the province for the nation,
the nation for all.

The devotee does not himself go to God.
If he did, he would not be able to bear
His dazzling light. Hence God Himself
comes down to His devotees and
appears to them in the form in which they
have adorned Him.

We do not have to seek an appointment
with Him for the hearing of our petition.
He hears the petitions of all
at the same time.

My patriotism is not an exclusive thing.
It is all-embracing and I should reject
that patriotism which seeks to mount
upon the distress or the exploitation
of other nationalities. The conception of
my patriotism is nothing if it is not always
in every case consistent with the broadest
good of humanity at large.

Absolute renunciation is not to be found
even on the peaks of the Himalayas.
The true cave is the one in the heart.
Man can hide himself within it and thus
protected can remain untouched
by the world.

There is a class of people [who] read
and read and read until they almost lose
their power of thinking. To such people
I suggest that they should stop reading
and think over what they have
previously read.

There are so many religions
as there are individuals.

Civilization is the mode of conduct
which points out to man the path of duty.

The tendency of the Indian civilization
is to elevate the moral being;
that of the Western civilization
is to propagate immortality.

To believe that what has not occurred in
history will not occur at all
is to argue disbelief in the dignity of man.

History is really a record
of every interruption of the even working
of the force of love or of the soul.

That nation is great which rests its head
upon death as its pillow.
Those who defy death
are free from all fear.

East and West can only really meet
when the West has thrown overboard
modern civilization.

Love is a rare herb that makes a friend
even of a sworn enemy
and this herb grows out of non-violence.

The force of love is the same as
the force of the soul or truth.
We have evidence of its working at every
step. The universe would disappear
without the existence of that force.

Chastity is one of the greatest disciplines without which the mind cannot attain requisite firmness.

Knowing the fundamentals, as I interpret it, means putting them into practice.

The first attribute of the divine heritage
is fearlessness.

I believe that all of us, individual souls,
living in this ocean of spirit,
are the same as one another
with the closest bond among ourselves.
A drop that separates soon dries up
and any soul that believes itself separate
from others is likewise destroyed.

The sum and substance of what I
want to say is that the individual person
should have control over the things
that are necessary for
the sustenance of life.

Ignorance will not disappear
merely with education. It can go only
with a change in our ways of thinking.

Literacy is necessary only to the extent that it develops our thinking power and teaches us to distinguish between good and evil.

Peace may arise out of strife, for all strife
is not antipacific.
To stand with folded hands
is not to achieve reform.

I want the freedom of my country
so that other countries
may learn something
from this country of mine.

Ours will only then be a truly spiritual
nation when we shall show more truth
than gold, greater fearlessness than
pomp of power and wealth,
greater charity than love of self.

Terrorize yourself; search within;
by all means resist tyranny wherever you
find it; by all means resist encroachment
upon your liberty, but not by shedding
blood of the tyrant.

We are not quite as free as we imagine.
Our past holds us.

Religion is the proper and eternal ally of art.

The central experience of life
will forever remain the relationship which
man has to God and it will never be
superseded or replaced by anything else.

What a joy it would be when people
realize that religion consists
not in outward ceremonial but an
ever-growing inward response to the
highest impulses man is capable of.

Religion is a thing to be lived.
It is not mere sophistry.

Eternal truth is one. God also is one.
Let every one of us steer clear of
conflicting creeds and customs and
follow the straight path of truth.

Brotherhood does not mean loving or sympathizing with those, extending the hand of fellowship to those who will in return love you. That is a bargain. Brotherhood is not a mercantile affair.

Prayer is a cry of the heart.
It can be fruitful if it comes from within.

For Hindus to expect Islam, Christianity or Zoroastrianism to be driven out of India is as idle a dream as it would be for Mussalmans to have only Islam of their imagination rule the world.

Truth is the exclusive property
of no single scripture.

Vanity is emptiness: self-respect is substance.

The purpose of life is undoubtedly
to know oneself. We cannot do it unless
we learn to identify ourselves with all that
lives. The sum total of that life is God.

Not to believe in the possibility of permanent peace is to disbelieve the godliness of human nature.

If even one great nation were
unconditionally to perform the supreme
act of renunciation, many of us would
see in our lifetime visible peace
established on earth.

Faith is not a thing to grasp, it is a state
to grow to. And growth
comes from within.

Generally history is the chronicle
of kings and their wars; the future history
will be the history of man.

Optimism indicates faith; only an atheist can be a pessimist.

Sorrow springs from dreaming of the
future and from lamenting the past.
Hence one who concerns himself with the
present and does his duty has neither
birth nor death.

It is our actions which count. Thoughts, however good in themselves, are like false pearls unless they are translated into action.

He who abides by the divine law will win bliss in this world, as also in the next. What is this divine law? It is that one has to suffer pain before enjoying pleasure and that one's true self-interest consists in the good of all, which means that we should die—suffer—for others.

A conscientious man hesitates to assert
himself, he is always humble,
never boisterous, always compromising,
always ready to listen, ever willing,
even anxious to admit mistakes.

The golden rule of conduct, therefore,
is mutual toleration, seeing that we will
never all think alike and that we shall
always see Truth in fragment
and from different angles of vision.

He alone is truly brave, he alone
is a martyr in the true sense
who dies without fear in his heart and
without wishing hurt to his enemy,
not the one who kills and dies.

A life wholly filled with the spirit of truth
should be clear and pure as crystal.

They [women] are labouring under the
hypnotic influence of man.

There is no limit to extending service to our neighbours across our State-made frontiers. God never made those frontiers.

Instead of saying God is Truth,
I say that Truth is God.

All our philosophy is in vain, if it does not enable us to rejoice in the company of fellow-beings and their service.

The way to Truth is paved with skeletons
over which we dare to walk.

He alone is a lover of Truth
who follows it in all conditions of life.

He [the wanted person] came and said
he believed in me and my teachings and
had decided to surrender himself. Even if
he had admitted his guilt to me I would
be bound not to disclose it to the police.
I could not be reformer and informer
at the same time.

Mahavira and Buddha were soldiers, and so was Tolstoy. Only they saw deeper and truer in their profession, and found the secret of a true, happy, honourable and godly life. Let us be joint sharers with these teachers and this land of ours will once more be the abode of gods.

Ahimsa is a great vow; it is more difficult than walking on the edge of a sword.

Anyone who desires to possess land
cannot practise ahimsa.

Ahimsa is a powerful emotion of the heart which finds expression in numerous forms of service. If it manifests itself in its perfection even in one human being, its light would be far more powerful than that of the sun.

The sine qua non of salvation
is a total annihilation of all desire.

Man is not to drown himself in the well of shastras but he is to dive into their broad ocean and bring out pearls.

The pathway of ahimsa, of love, one has often to tread all alone.

What a wife who refuses to submit to a
cruel husband does, constitutes
non-violent non-cooperation.

The path of Truth
is the path of non-violence.

Non-violence is a weapon of the strong.

I am not a visionary. I claim to be
a practical idealist.

Love has no boundary. My nationalism includes the love of all the nations of the earth irrespective of creed.

Forgiveness is a quality of the soul.

Truth to me is infinitely dearer than the `mahatmaship', which is purely a burden. It is my knowledge of my limitations and my nothingness which has so far saved me from the oppressivenes of the `mahatmaship'.

Love is not love which asks for a return.

When the sense of `I' has vanished, we
cease to feel that we are subject to
anyone's authority.

We should not feel unhappy if on some occasion we commit an error. We should feel unhappy only if in committing it we had willingly yielded to a weakness in us or had not been vigilant enough, if we had not struggled to overcome it.

The attainment of freedom, whether for a man, a nation or the world, must be in exact proportion to the attainment of non-violence by each.

Only when the least can say, `I have got my liberty', have I got mine.

It gives me ineffable joy to make experiments proving that love is the supreme and the only law of life.

Secrecy is a sin and symptom of violence, and therefore, to be avoided, especially if the freedom of the dumb millions is the goal.

It is man's imagination that divides the world into warring groups of enemies and friends. In the ultimate resort, it is the power of love that acts even in the midst of the clash and sustains the world.

My faith is the brightest in the midst of impenetrable darkness.

One of the axioms of religion is: there is
no religion other than Truth.
Another is: religion is love.

The struggle of non-violence against violence, no matter from what quarter the latter comes, must continue till a single representative is left alive. More, no man can do; to do less would be tantamount to want of faith.

Beauty because of its quality of
inwardness cannot be experienced
in the physical sense.

True education is that which helps us
to know the atman, our true self,
God and Truth.

True development consists in reducing ourselves to a cipher.

Selfless service is the secret of life.
To rise above passions
is the highest ideal.

Sanyas does not mean the renunciation
of all activities; it means only
the renunciation of activities prompted by
desire and of the fruits of
action performed as duty.

A guru is one who guides us to
righteousness by his own
righteous conduct.

Independent India, as conceived by me, will have all Indians belonging to different religions living in perfect friendship. There will be no millionaires and no paupers; all would belong to the State, for the State belonged to them.

Only the self-reliant man can progress towards success in any task. This is as true of a country as of a man.

Sadhus should not do anything
which would harm the people. Let society
never encourage them to do so.

It is very difficult—practically impossible—to achieve real freedom without self-denial.

Non-cooperation is a protest against an unwitting and unwilling participation in evil.

I have conceived no such thing as Gandhism. I am not an exponent of any sect. I never claimed to have originated any philosophy.

I am not anti-English; I am not anti-British; I am not `anti' any government; I am anti-untruth, anti-humbug and anti-injustice.

I want no revolution. I want
ordered progress. I want no disordered
order. I want no chaos.
I want real order to be evolved out of this
chaos which is misrepresented to me
as order.

Education, character and religion
should be regarded as convertible terms.

Every religion in some measure satisfies
the spiritual needs of men.

My experiment in non-violence
would be instantly successful
if I could secure women's help.

Kindness should be exercised
for the sake of kindness; the reward
will then come unsought.

A girl who wishes to remain unmarried
should be wedded to independence.
A girl dependent upon others can never
remain unmarried.

If an ancestral treasure lying buried in a corner of the house unknown to the members of the family were suddenly discovered, what a celebration it would occasion. Similarly, women's marvellous power is lying dormant. If the women of Asia wake up, they will dazzle the world.

A man should remain man and yet
should become woman; similarly,
a woman should remain woman and yet
become man. This means that man
should cultivate the gentleness and the
discrimination of woman; and woman
should cast off her timidity and become
brave and courageous.

Only the self can raise the self;
the self is the help of the self.
Only women can raise women.

It is possible and necessary to treat
human beings on terms of equality,
but this can never apply to their morals.

Men generally hesitate to make a
beginning if they feel that the objective
cannot be had in its entirety.
Such an attitude of mind is in reality
a bar to progress.

Max Mueller put the spirit of Hinduism in a nutshell when he said: `India considers life as only one thing—duty—whereas others think of enjoyment cum duty.'

There can be no living harmony between
races and nations unless the main cause
is removed—namely,
exploitation of the weak by the strong.

I believe in the rock-bottom doctrine of
Advaita and my interpretation of Advaita
excludes totally any idea of superiority at
any stage.

I believe implicitly
that all men are born equal.

A life of sacrifice is the pinnacle of art
and is full of true joy.

All rights to be deserved and preserved
come from duty well done.

The real implication of equal distribution is that each man shall have the wherewithal to supply all his natural needs and no more.

To say it is impossible because it is difficult is not in consonance with the spirit of the age. Things undreamt of are daily being seen, the impossible is ever becoming possible.

To try to root out religion itself from society is a wild goose chase. And were such an attempt to succeed, it would mean the destruction of society.

I hate privilege and monopoly.
Whatever cannot be shared with the
masses is taboo to me.

Compromise comes in at every step, but one must realize that it is a compromise and keep the final goal constantly in front of the mind's eye.

All the graces of life are possible
only when we learn the art
of living nobly.

Sometimes good comes out of evil,
but that is divine dispensation.

The masses have no other knowledge but experience to guide them.

To those who are hungry and unemployed, God can dare reveal Himself only as work and wages as the assurance of food.

We shall never be able to raise the standard of public life through laws.

Is not politics too a part of dharma?
Politics requires purity of conduct.

What we mean by independence
is that we will not live on the sufferance
of any people on earth.

My life is my message.